Effects of Alcoholism

Knowing The Effects of Alcohol and it's Control Mechanisms

Flawless Dave

Table of Contents

Why do people drink?

This is due to the high consumption of alcohol in our general public. It has been a piece of the human experience starting from the start. It used to be something that individuals put their lives in extreme danger to make, sell and drink, however today we have the advantage of buying it at service stations, supermarkets, and alcohol stores stacked with containers of every conceivable assortment.

We never again need to speed serious areas of strength down since we have a large number of various wines and, surprisingly, dessert wine coolers, margaritas, and frozen drinks.

Things being what they are, the reason in all actuality do individuals drink alcohol today? Is it unique concerning the reasons individuals savored the times of running homebrew?

For some grown-ups, alcohol is a pleasurable method for denoting the most significant snapshots of life. Consider a dad toasting his little girl the day he strolls her down the passageway.

Truly mind-blowing features can be set apart by a beverage or two and it is totally solid. A few beverages like red wine could have some medical advantages. It is when alcohol turns out to be too significant in day-to-day existence that it tips the line toward undesirable.

Alcohol can deliver a scope of outcomes to the focal sensory system, including diminished hindrance. It is likewise a depressant, and that implies it dials back the body's capabilities.

Alcohol additionally significantly affects synapses in the cerebrum, which are synthetic substances that permit nerve cells to speak with each other.

Quite possibly of the most notable synapse, serotonin can be impacted by alcohol utilization. This might prompt sensations of discouragement and nervousness. Alcohol can likewise cause liver harm and different sicknesses, so it is essential to dependably consume.

The sign is that we use it broadly in friendly settings. The cerebrum's endorphin framework is set off by liquor. Endorphins structure some portion of the cerebrum's aggravation alleviating framework, and they are delivered in light of torment. On account of alcohol, this implies that when we feel torment, we discharge a greater amount of these narcotics than we would on the off chance that we were not encountering torment by any stretch of the imagination.

At the end of the day, alcohol exacerbates us. For this reason, halting drinking is so troublesome. It is likewise why individuals who have been drinking for quite a while are bound to become more dependent on alcohol than the people who are simply beginning on the way to collectedness. Drinking alcohol can likewise be a strategy for dealing with especially difficult times for certain individuals. They might be discouraged or have low confidence and drinking is a method for getting away from the real world.

Others might involve alcohol as a prize framework in the wake of really buckling down for quite a long time. Others drink since they are exhausted or discontent with their life. In conclusion, many individuals drink since it permits them to be social with their companions.

Previous Experiences

It is normal for heavy drinkers to have experienced childhood in a family with a drunkard and never figured out how to adapt to their feelings so they go to alcohol, the same way they were in a roundabout way educated.

They might have been harassed while growing up and gone to liquor as a strategy for dealing with especially difficult times since it seemed like they were in charge.

A horrendous mishap can make a singular go-to liquor a method for desensitizing the torment. These are only a couple of instances of how previous encounters can lead individuals down the way of alcohol addiction.

Drunkards could have a horrendous youth and they drink to get away from the aggravation. Alcohol will numb them and they won't feel anything. They could have been mishandled as a youngster and for reasons unknown, they think drinking is the best way to adapt to it.

Many individuals could feel like they need alcohol to assist them with easier thinking about themselves or something in their life. Drunkards probably won't know how to manage what they are feeling so they drink all things being equal.

Certain individuals could drink as a result of how they were raised, yet I don't completely accept that everybody turns into a drunkard in light of what occurred previously.

Stress

One of the many reasons that individuals go to alcohol is to assist them with adapting to pressure. Stress prompts a wide range of medical conditions, and during distressing times, individuals will frequently go to alcohol as an approach to adapting.

This can prompt alcohol dependence. At the point when somebody has an alcohol dependence, they can't quit drinking despite the unfavorable impacts that it has on their wellbeing and prosperity. The individual may likewise encounter withdrawal side effects when they quit drinking for even a brief timeframe.

To Socialize

There is a great deal of examination about how mingling can make individuals become heavy drinkers. AA has a colloquialism "The main prerequisite for participation is a craving to quit drinking."

This implies that drunkards don't have to drink to be individuals from AA, they simply need the longing to quit drinking.

This appears to be legit because mingling and alcohol make a perfect fit. It's difficult to go out without being offered drinks.

That's what certain individuals say "social consumers" exist, however they're simply the ones who limit their admission or take drinks with food.

Seeing the relationship amongst mingling and alcoholism is hard not. Research has found that the individuals who associate something like once each week are at a lot higher gamble of turning into a drunkard than the people who just beverage from time to time.

The more frequently individuals drink, the more probable it is that they will foster an issue with alcohol.

Climate

The climate individuals live in can be a reason for alcohol addiction. For instance, on the off chance that individuals live in a space where they have closeness to alcohol merchants, this makes it more straightforward for them to buy alcohol. This could prompt alcohol addiction since there is a greater chance for them to drink.

Easy Access

Easy access to alcohol is a hypothesis that recommends that the more helpful it is for individuals to purchase alcohol, the more probable they are to drink.

Consequences of this hypothesis have been blended, as certain examinations have found that comfort doesn't assume a critical part in alcohol use. Notwithstanding, it has been shown that those with admittance to alcohol will quite often drink more than the individuals who don't have this accommodation.

The Causes of Alcohol Addiction

Part of the explanation that such countless individuals foster alcohol dependence is that they accept that drinking alcohol assists them with adapting to their sentiments. At the point when they are feeling worried, miserable, or restless, they might go to alcohol as an approach to adapting to these sentiments. Many individuals imagine that alcohol will assist them with adapting better compared to different substances.

As a general rule, be that as it may, alcohol expands nervousness and discouragement, and it causes sensations of disconnection and dismissal. It is entirely expected for individuals with a dependence on alcohol to encounter self-destructive contemplations when they quit drinking for a while.

One more motivation behind why certain individuals become dependent on alcohol is a direct result of how it causes them to feel. They could appreciate time with companions more while they're drinking, for instance. Certain individuals additionally accept that alcohol can assist them with feeling more sure and along these lines have the option to meet new individuals or join bunches all the more without any problem.

Be that as it may, this isn't generally the situation. Some of the time individuals who drink an excessive amount will become disconnected from loved ones as a result of their enslavement and their powerlessness to control their drinking propensities.

Rather than resting easier thinking about themselves in the wake of drinking a lot at gatherings or get-togethers, people who disapprove of alcohol addiction frequently have a more regrettable outlook on themselves after such occasions since they can't quit drinking notwithstanding the pessimistic outcomes it has caused in their lives.

Alcohol addiction is a movement and there's an "endless loop" related to over-the-top drinking, with much to lose en route on the off chance that individuals don't look for help. The bend demonstrates the way that life can deteriorate on the off chance that the pattern of reliance isn't broken, however, it can likewise help better through recuperation.

Pre-Alcoholic

During the pre-alcoholic stage, there is little proof of issue drinking. The first includes general trial and error with alcohol and is when alcohol resilience creates as the individual starts drinking all the more consistently as a survival technique for nervousness, stress, or different feelings

Beginning phase

This is the momentary stage where the improvement of an example of alcohol abuse begins. Drinking turns out to be more customary, and people start blaming get-togethers to drink. They may likewise begin polishing off alcohol to adapt to the unfortunate results brought about by drinking like headaches.

Center Stage

This is the most significant stage and when an individual starts to drink as often as possible and reliably, perhaps getting going their day with a beverage. They might battle with deteriorating associations with loved ones or experience changes to their way of behaving that influence them adversely. They frequently experience well-being influences related to weighty drinking, for example, headaches or feeling debilitated more frequently than while not drinking

Late Stage

This last stage prompts a total loss of command over alcohol utilization — where the individual feels they should drink. Right now, the singular's body starts to require the presence of alcohol to feel ordinary, known as reliance. At the point when the individual doesn't polish off alcohol consistently, they might encounter withdrawal side effects and powerful desires.

Effects of alcohol on a person's behavior

Although it very well may be challenging to detect, there are various normal ways of behaving imparted by people to alcohol addiction. Alcohol addiction is generally difficult to distinguish in individuals, however for somebody near a heavy drinker, changes in conduct are much of the time a warning.

While alcohol addiction doesn't have a sort, and anybody can be impacted by the infection of alcohol addiction, there are a couple of key ways of behaving that are unmistakable when an individual is battling with a liquor use jumble.

Alcoholic way of behaving is some of the time alluded to as an alcoholic character. This doesn't imply that an individual has a character that gets them in a position to turn into a heavy drinker.

Saying that somebody has a heavy drinker character is simply one more approach to saying that an individual is acting such that individuals battling with alcohol addiction ordinarily act.

Understanding these ways of behaving may help a friend or family member who is worried about the drinking propensities for somebody they care about.

Unexpected Anger or Unprovoked Aggression

Alcohol changes the cerebrum, and when an individual is reliant or dependent, the individual will encounter withdrawal side effects without alcohol. This is because of a substance's lopsidedness because of the absence of alcohol. Subsequently, they might encounter desires that can set off a forceful reaction.

Individuals may likewise turn out to be exceptionally forceful when they are inebriated. Alcohol might influence how individuals respond to their current circumstances making a forceful reaction when set off.

Something as minor as a terrible day, a misspoken word, or on the other hand on the off chance that an individual is holding onto repressed dissatisfactions could bring about a contention. Some of the time individuals are for the most part furious, and when they drink unnecessarily it turns out in additional extraordinary ways. It is generally difficult to sort out what the impacts of alcohol will be on an individual who manhandles liquor.

Alcoholic Blackouts

At the point when an individual encounters a power outage, they can't remember what occurred while they were drinking. This is because of over-the-top alcohol utilization, similar to hitting the bottle hard. The cerebrum is inebriated to such an extent that it can't store recollections, so recollections of occasions that happen during a power outage are lost to the individual drinking.

During these power outages, an individual might lose hindrances, direct criminal behavior, get into contentions or even actual viciousness, really hurt themselves, or even drive inebriated.

The individual is additionally in danger of being physically attacked, winding up someplace without really any information on how they arrived, or another sort of risk.

Regardless of whether an individual is sufficiently fortunate to not have an adverse occasion occur during a power outage, it is as yet a disturbing event. Shutting down in a real sense makes an individual's cerebrum breakdowns to the place where it isn't equipped for quite possibly of its most considered normal capability.

Individuals experiencing alcohol addiction are substantially more defenseless against power outages and may have them consistently. You might see it difficult for them to review things that happened the prior night while they were drinking. They may likewise much of the time drop following an evening of drinking.

Powerlessness to Stop Drinking

People that don't tend to drink too much don't
battle to distinguish the line between when
they need to quit drinking.

**Individuals with AUD can't recognize
that line.**

People who are addicted to alcohol honestly
and rationally feel the urge to drink.. These
alcohol desires can be serious areas of
strength extraordinarily while they are
drinking. Some could try and portray these
sentiments as having become intellectually
fixated on drinking.

As a result of these physical and mental
longings, a heavy drinker is frequently
incapable to stop, whether it be for the
afternoon, the week, the month, or the year.

Some essentially probably shouldn't quit drinking.

Talking, for the most part, numerous people with an alcohol use jumble show ways of behaving that are coldhearted, misdirecting, and guileful.

While these ways of behaving are not viewed as certain, they don't imply that a heavy drinker is a terrible individual. What this demonstrates is that they have a sickness that constrains them to act in some ways to satisfy their desires for alcohol.

A few extra characteristics that are found in an individual with an alcohol use jumble include:

- manipulative
- clandestine
- exceptionally worried about the picture

- unfortunate mental self-portrait
- delicate
- pointless
- restless
- protective
- low-confidence
- disconnected
- bad-tempered

Since these ways of behaving are because of a need-driven impulse to drink, the new ways of behaving may push out the character of the individual they were previously. It can prompt critical issues in an individual's private and expert life.

Effects of alcohol on emotions

Individuals might utilize alcohol to adapt to close-to-home agony or work in friendly working, however, its misuse can exacerbate profound and social issues. The close-to-home impacts of alcohol can be serious areas of strength for particularly individuals who have a current mental or actual medical issue. Over the long haul, be that as it may, alcohol can exacerbate these circumstances.

Alcohol also influences the cerebrum's cerebral cortex, which is where thought handling and cognizance happen. Alcohol utilization, particularly in enormous amounts, slows down a levelheaded idea. Drinking likewise pushes down the conduct inhibitory focuses, making an individual have less restraint and show more unfortunate judgment. This absence of hindrance frequently drives individuals to drink more than they in any case would.

While you might feel significantly better for some time in the wake of polishing off alcohol, the impacts are consistently impermanent. An individual might feel good feelings while impaired, however, the close-to-home factors that prompted alcohol misuse to stay after the inebriation blurs.

Alcohol Numbness

Individuals battling close-to-home torment might drink alcohol to accomplish a condition of deadness. Given the impacts of inebriation, accomplishing impermanent deadness by drinking is conceivable. Over-the-top alcohol utilization could prompt power outages and omissions in memory.

While shutting down can unquestionably assist an individual with accomplishing a condition of deadness, toasting the place of a power outage is hazardous. During a power outage, an individual fails to keep a grip on driving forces and experiences issues with levelheaded independent direction. This improves the probability of hazardous exercises, like driving impaired or having unprotected sex. The condition of deadness that accompanies over-the-top liquor utilization is offset by the dangers that show up with it.

Emotional Flatness

Since alcohol expands GABA levels, drinking can relaxingly affect the body. Subsequently, certain individuals might utilize alcohol to quiet their feelings, however, these quieting impacts are additionally impermanent.

On the off chance that an individual expands their alcohol use over the long haul and fosters resilience, it will take more noteworthy measures of alcohol to accomplish similar quieting impacts. At the point when an individual with alcohol resilience quits drinking or attempts to scale back, they might encounter withdrawal side effects because their body is utilized to the presence of alcohol and its consequences for GABA levels. Without the alcohol expected to expand GABA levels, the body goes through withdrawal, prompting side effects like nervousness.

At last, the close-to-home levelness that accompanies alcohol misuse vanishes, and it turns out to be significantly more enthusiastically for an individual to control their feelings.

Alcohol addiction and Emotional Abuse

Alcohol enslavement can cause serious disturbance in private connections and families. During a time of inebriation, an individual's feelings are some of the time crude and untrustworthy, bringing about outrage, episodes of craziness, crying fits, or even physical or boisterous attacks. This leads others to keep away from the person out of dread or because of their powerlessness to adapt.

The individual mishandling alcohol is frequently viewed as being deceitful, effortlessly incited, temperamental, and contemptible of regard. Tragically, these are much of the time a portion of the feelings that lead to alcohol maltreatment in any case. Subsequently, the pattern of misuse proceeds and feeds into itself.

Individuals with an alcohol use jumble show specific side effects, for example, proceeding to drink in any event, when it influences physical and psychological well-being or brings on some issues in associations with loved ones. At the end of the day, the issues an individual attempt to fix with alcohol may deteriorate as enslavement creates.

Other long-haul outcomes of alcohol misuse incorporate social issues, issues with learning and memory, and psychological well-being issues like discouragement and nervousness. Generally speaking, alcohol adversely affects mental and close-to-home wellbeing, regardless of whether it briefly numbs feelings or makes sensations of happiness.

Alcohol issues and mental medical affliction are firmly connected. Individuals who drink a ton of alcohol are bound to foster psychological well-being issues. It's likewise a fact that individuals with serious mental chronic sickness are bound to have alcohol issues. This might be because they 'self-sedate', meaning they drink to manage troublesome sentiments or side effects.

Alcohol and discouragement

Customary weighty drinking is connected to the side effects of discouragement. Frequently, individuals with discouragement who drink alcohol will find they begin to feel significantly improved inside the initial not many long stretches of halting drinking. On the off chance that you attempt this and feel significantly improved, it's reasonable that the alcohol was causing your downturn. On the off chance that your side effects of discouragement proceed, address your GP for help.

It's for the most part not prescribed to drink on the off chance that you're taking antidepressants. Alcohol can exacerbate discouragement and increment the symptoms of certain antidepressants. On the off chance that you're attempting to chop down or quit drinking, research shows a few antidepressants can expand your gamble of backsliding.

Alcohol and nervousness

On the off chance that you experience nervousness, alcohol can provide you with an exceptionally fleeting sensation of unwinding - however, this rapidly vanishes. On the off chance that you depend on alcohol to cover your nervousness, you may before long wind up drinking increasingly more to unwind. After some time, this can prompt alcohol reliance.

You may likewise find a headache exacerbates your nervousness.

On the off chance that you use alcohol to loosen up, contemplate alternate ways you can find to unwind: reflection, yoga, exercise, or setting aside a few minutes for things you appreciate, for instance.

Alcohol and psychosis

It's feasible to encounter psychosis on the off chance that you consistently drink a great deal of alcohol, or on the other hand on the off chance that you're a weighty consumer and out of nowhere quit drinking.

Alcohol, self-destruction, and self-hurt

Since alcohol can cause you to lose your restraints and act all the more incautiously, it might prompt activities like self-mischief or self-destruction. Weighty drinking is additionally connected to self-destructive considerations and endeavors.

Control of alcoholism

On the off chance that you or somebody you care about definitely disapproves of liquor enslavement, it very well might be an ideal opportunity to look for proficient assistance. Research has demonstrated the way that restoration treatment can be exceptionally compelling in assisting people with keeping an existence of collectedness.

When balanced out, the objective is to progress from detox to treatment, to support (rehearsing sober carrying on with by completely changing you), to amazing quality — the last move toward the way to recuperation.

Perceiving the side effects of alcohol addiction can have a colossal effect on seeking legitimate treatment and heading down the way to recuperation. A few admonition signs include:

•	Drinking more than arranged or expected

•	Neglecting to satisfy commitments at school, work, or home (focusing on drinking, notwithstanding obligations, prompting missed everyday schedule)

•   Proceeding to use notwithstanding adverse consequences on connections, monetary circumstance, or wellbeing

•   Involving in circumstances that could be genuinely dangerous, such as driving drunk

•   Showing an expanded resilience to alcohol (savoring more requests to accomplish a similar wanted impact). Since the cerebrum changes with alcohol misuse, one of the principal physiological indications of enslavement is developing resilience.

•   Encountering physical or mental withdrawal side effects while endeavoring to quit drinking (nervousness, discouragement, a sleeping disorder, queasiness, perspiring, hand quakes/"the shakes," disarray, seizures, and visual mind flights)

•   Losing interest in once-delighted exercises or turning out to be socially disconnected

•   Becoming untrustworthy or clandestine, forceful, ill-humored, or unpredictable — individuals who have liquor enslavement will attempt to conceal it.

- Hankering liquor, like drinking first thing

- Investing an unreasonable measure of energy contemplating drinking, obtaining liquor, and recuperating from headaches

Tracking down Detox and Treatment

There are numerous ways of getting level-headed and nobody's "right" way. The initial step is tracking down a trustworthy alcohol or other illicit drug use treatment supplier. You'll need to find a therapy clinic that has therapeutically regulated detox capacities so you can serenely and securely detox from alcohol. There are long-term and short-term choices, however, an enslavement expert ought to decide the best degree of care for you in light of your singular requirements. Successful enslavement treatment suppliers will have dependent instructors, however, they ought to likewise have psychological well-being administrations as many individuals with liquor addiction have co-happening psychological well-being conditions.

Methodologies for Dealing with Alcohol Use Disorder: What to Say and Do

Endeavoring to help a friend or family member or companion who is battling an alcohol use confusion can be a close-to-home exciting ride. At the point when a heavy drinker is in dynamic enslavement, they can be protective. Try not to go up against the ways of behaving while they're inebriated. Figure out an opportunity when they're level-headed and discuss your interests. Practice what you will say. Don't manipulate or relegate fault; this is an infection. Offer help and use articulations beginning with "I, for example,

- I see ...

- I feel ...

- I trust and expect ...

- I will ...

- I'm worried about you because...

Make a move. Track down help for you and other relatives, as well. Figure out how to define solid limits for yourself. By the day's end, the individual with enslavement must acknowledge help.

www.ingramcontent.com/pod-product-compliance
Lightning Source LLC
Chambersburg PA
CBHW071501150726
48000CB00006B/2664